DETROIT
TIGERS

by Joanne C. Gerstner

Published by ABDO Publishing Company, 8000 West 78th Street, Edina, Minnesota 55439. Copyright © 2011 by Abdo Consulting Group, Inc. International copyrights reserved in all countries. No part of this book may be reproduced in any form without written permission from the publisher. SportsZone™ is a trademark and logo of ABDO Publishing Company.

Printed in the United States of America,
North Mankato, Minnesota
112010
012011

 THIS BOOK CONTAINS AT LEAST 10% RECYCLED MATERIALS.

Editor: Chrös McDougall
Copy Editor: Nicholas Cafarelli
Interior Design and Production: Christa Schneider
Cover Design: Christa Schneider

Photo Credits: Mark Duncan/AP Images, cover, 31; AP Images, 1, 14, 17, 19, 20, 23, 26, 42 (top and bottom), 44; Amy Sancetta/AP Images, 4, 43 (bottom); Jeff Roberson/AP Images, 7; Library of Congress, 8, 11, 13, 42 (middle); Focus On Sport/Getty Images, 25; Walter Iooss Jr./Sports Illustrated/Getty Images, 29; Ron Heflin/AP Images, 33, 43 (top); John Swart/AP Images, 34; Duane Burleson/AP Images, 37, 43 (middle); Paul Sancya/AP Images, 39; Jim Mone/ AP Images, 41; Carlos Osorio/AP Images, 47

Library of Congress Cataloging-in-Publication Data
Gerstner, Joanne, 1971-
  Detroit Tigers / by Joanne Gerstner.
     p. cm. — (Inside MLB)
  Includes index.
  ISBN 978-1-61714-043-3
  1. Detroit Tigers (Baseball team)—History—Juvenile literature. I. Title.
  GV875.D6G47 2011
  796.357'640977434—dc22
                          2010036562

TABLE OF CONTENTS

CHAPTER 1

RESTORING THE ROAR

O n a beautiful October afternoon in 2006, fans filled Comerica Park in Detroit for a special day of baseball. The fans could barely stay in their seats. The Detroit Tigers were hosting the Oakland Athletics in the American League Championship Series (ALCS). The Tigers led the series 3–0. With one more win, they would advance to the World Series for the first time since 1984.

The game stayed close throughout. With two outs in the bottom of the ninth inning, the Tigers and A's were tied at 3–3. Two runners were on base as Tigers outfielder Magglio Ordonez stepped to the plate. With a base hit, the Tigers would be going to the World Series. With an out, they would go to extra innings.

Ordonez was one of the top batters for the Tigers in 2006. He had hit .298 with 24 home runs and 104 runs batted in (RBIs) that season. He had

Magglio Ordonez celebrates his three-run homer as he runs around the bases. The home run sent the Tigers to the 2006 World Series.

already hit a home run in this game. When he saw a pitch he liked, he hit another one. Just like that, the Tigers won 6–3.

The fans went wild. Ordonez raised his arms above his head while he jumped and skipped around the bases. When he arrived at home plate, the entire Tigers team grabbed him in a big hug.

The Tigers have a long history in Major League Baseball (MLB). But in 2003, they lost 119 games. That was the worst in team history. One more loss would have tied them for the worst record in major league history.

Tigers' fans were very embarrassed by all of the losing. The once-proud team had become a national joke.

But the Tigers avoided that 120th loss. Three years later, they were back among the top teams in baseball.

The Tigers' dream 2006 season ended at the World Series. They made eight errors against the National League (NL) champion St. Louis Cardinals in the World Series. That was the most in World Series history.

The pitchers had the most trouble. They committed a World Series-record five errors. Pitchers Justin Verlander and Fernando Rodney struggled fielding bunts and throwing to first base. Their throws were wild and the errors proved

Still the Worst

The New York Mets finished an MLB-worst 40–120 in their first season, 1962. No other MLB team has lost that many games in a season. But the 2003 Detroit Tigers came close. The Tigers had 118 losses with six games still to play. They looked like they would tie or break the record. But they won five out of their last six games to avoid being a bad part of baseball history.

After a great regular season, outfielder Curtis Granderson and the Tigers struggled in the 2006 World Series.

costly. The Cardinals beat the Tigers four games to one.

Although the Tigers did not win the World Series, the fans in Detroit were still happy. After all, their team was winning once again. And, with a young team, the Tigers appeared ready to keep winning.

The Tigers had brought in established veterans like Ordonez, pitcher Kenny Rogers, catcher Ivan Rodriguez, and shortstop Carlos Guillen. They teamed with young players such as pitchers Verlander and Jeremy Bonderman and out-fielder Curtis Granderson to create a solid core.

The Tigers again showed a commitment to winning. The proud tradition that is Detroit Tigers baseball lived on.

CHAPTER 2

FROM WOLVERINES TO TIGERS

Baseball has been a big part of life in Detroit for more than 100 years. The sport has been played professionally in the city since 1879.

The Detroit Tigers have become more than the city's baseball team. They have been a source of pride for winning 10 American League (AL) pennants and four World Series titles. And at times, the Tigers have been an embarrassment for losing too many games.

Songs have been written about the team. The famous Tigers Old English D logo has appeared in movies, television shows, and music videos.

The Famous "D"

The Detroit Tigers Old English D logo on their caps and jerseys has also become a symbol for the city. The main character in a popular television show during the 1980s, Magnum P.I., often wore a Tigers baseball cap. Detective Thomas Magnum, played by actor Tom Selleck, wore a Tigers hat even though the show was set in Hawaii. Selleck grew up in suburban Detroit and chose to wear the hat to honor the Tigers—his favorite baseball team. The Tigers baseball cap has also been made popular by Detroit musicians Eminem and Kid Rock.

Detroit Wolverines outfielder Ned Hanlon poses for a portrait around 1887. He played for the Wolverines from 1881 to 1888.

Professional baseball started in the Motor City on May 12, 1879. That is when a team from Detroit played a team from Troy, New York, as part of the National Professional Baseball Players league. The Detroit team soon adopted a nickname, the Wolverines. The name honored Michigan's official state animal.

The original Wolverines team folded during the 1879 season. However, a different club named the Wolverines was successful after joining the National League in 1881. They even won the 1887 World Series, which was a forerunner of the modern MLB championship. The Wolverines beat the St. Louis Browns, 10 games to 5.

The Wolverines were sold after winning the Series. New owner George Arthur Vanderbeck changed the team's name from the Wolverines to the Creams. They also joined the minor league Western League.

The Creams played baseball on various fields around Detroit until 1896. That is when the team developed a permanent baseball home called Bennett Park. The Creams also took on a new nickname that season: the Tigers.

Bennett Park's field would serve the team for the next 104 years, expanding and changing

Charlie Bennett

Charlie Bennett is credited with inventing the chest protector, the shield worn by catchers over their torsos. He had 654 hits, 37 home runs, and 353 RBIs in 625 games played in eight years with the Wolverines. He died in 1927, in Detroit, at the age 72.

This portrait shows Wolverines catcher Charlie Bennett in 1887. The team later renamed its home ballpark after Bennett.

as the Tigers and the game of baseball grew. It would eventually be known as Tiger Stadium.

The original stadium was named after catcher Charlie Bennett. He had played for the Wolverines for eight seasons, starting in 1881. He later played for the Boston Beaneaters until a train accident ended his career in 1893. Bennett moved back to Detroit and was embraced by Tigers fans after his accident. He threw out the first pitch on each Opening Day from 1901 through 1926.

The Tigers joined the newly formed AL in October 1900. They played their first game on April 25, 1901. The Tigers beat the Milwaukee Brewers, 14–13, in front of 10,023 fans at Bennett Park.

Soon, a bigger stadium was built around the playing field. Tigers games became the popular place in the city to go for fun. Baseball games in Detroit had a carnival-like atmosphere. Elaborate parades were held to celebrate Opening Day. The outfield walls were colorful, filled with advertisements for clothing, soda, taxi services, and other products.

Fans even built their own bleachers outside the outfield walls of Bennett Park, called "wildcat bleachers." They were not official seats, but offered a great view of the field from

Wildcat Bleachers

Wildcat bleachers are stands built outside of a stadium. A modern version of wildcat bleachers can be seen on the rooftops of apartment buildings that surround the outfield sections of Wrigley Field in Chicago. The owners of the buildings sell their own tickets for Chicago Cubs games. The homeowners around Bennett Park charged five cents per ticket to watch Tigers games from their wildcat bleachers. The wildcat bleachers were taken down in 1911 when the stadium was expanded.

Sam Crawford, shown around 1913, joined the Tigers in 1903. He led the AL in triples five times during his 15 seasons in Detroit.

people's front and back yards. "Wildcat fans," as they became known, tended to be rowdy and turned the games into a party.

Despite the fan support, the Tigers were just a mediocre team in their early years. During their first six seasons, the Tigers' best finish was third place out of eight teams. They did that both in 1901 and 1905. But that was about to change.

Detroit had its baseball team, a permanent place to play, and soon the city would be home to baseball's first superstar: Ty Cobb.

CHAPTER 3

TY COBB, THEN A TITLE

Thousands of players have played in the major leagues, but few had the abilities of Tigers star Ty Cobb. The player who would later be known as "The Genius on Spikes" began playing with the Tigers at the end of the 1905 season. He was only 18 years old when he debuted. Nobody could have imagined the teenager from Georgia would soon become baseball's best player.

Cobb was a great hitter who could play in the outfield or infield. He also was a very fast runner and loved baseball strategy. However, Cobb was also known for his quick, mean temper. It often got him in trouble. He started fights with teammates. Sometimes he even fought with fans who yelled at him from the stands.

In 1907, Cobb got into big trouble. He was angry about the condition of the outfield during spring training. Tigers catcher Charlie "Boss" Schmidt

Nicknamed the "Georgia Peach," Ty Cobb established himself as one of the greatest hitters of all time during his 22 seasons with the Tigers.

stopped Cobb from fighting with a stadium groundskeeper. Cobb then became angry with Schmidt.

Cobb stayed mad. He picked another fight with Schmidt a few weeks later. Schmidt, who was much bigger than Cobb, easily won the fight. He left Cobb with a broken nose and two black eyes along with a lot of bruises. Tigers manager Hughie Jennings was upset with his players.

"You may have killed, or probably ruined forever, the greatest ballplayer in the world," Jennings told the team. ". . . Without him, we have no chance to be anywhere in the pennant race."

Jennings asked the players to apologize to Cobb, and he soon became better friends with his teammates. It was a good thing that he did. Cobb played for the Tigers from 1905 until 1926. He set many records that stand to this day.

His lifetime batting average of .367 is the highest in major league history. He won the batting title 12 times. He also had 4,191 hits during his career. That stood as an MLB record until Pete Rose broke it in September 1985.

Cobb's influence helped turn the Tigers from a mediocre team to the top team in the AL. Detroit won the AL pennant

Ty Cobb slides into third base. He stole a career-high 96 bases in 1915 and led the AL in stolen bases six times.

in 1907, 1908, and 1909. But Cobb could not help the Tigers win the World Series. They lost each year, twice to the Chicago Cubs and once to the Pittsburgh Pirates.

The Tigers were often a winning team during the remainder of Cobb's career. He even was named AL Most Valuable Player (MVP) in 1911. But Cobb and the Tigers did not win

any more pennants. Cobb also became the Tigers' manager from 1921 to 1926. It was not uncommon for a player to also serve as a coach or manager during that time. But Cobb left the Tigers after the 1926 season. He would not be the last superstar Tiger, however.

The team soon added right fielder Harry Heilmann, catcher Mickey Cochrane,

MOVING ON UP

Due to stars like Ty Cobb and three AL pennants, the Tigers became wildly popular in Detroit during the early 1900s. As such, the team's owners gradually made the stadium bigger. Bennett Park was the Tigers' first home. The stadium was outside of downtown and had wooden bleachers that held 10,000 fans. In 1912, owner Frank Navin decided to build a new stadium on the same site. This one was made of concrete and steel so it could hold more fans. The new stadium, called Navin Field, held 23,000.

New team owner Walter Briggs added a second level to the stadium in 1935, allowing a total of 53,000 fans to watch games. The ballpark was renamed Briggs Stadium in 1938, and then Tiger Stadium in 1961. Not much was done to the stadium in the following years. It closed in 1999 and the Tigers moved into the newly built Comerica Park in downtown Detroit in 2000.

second baseman Charlie Gehringer, infielder/outfielder Hank Greenberg, and pitcher Goose Goslin. And they managed to accomplish something Cobb could not: win the World Series.

The Tigers had won the 1934 AL pennant but lost to the St. Louis Cardinals in the World Series. Then they won the AL pennant again in 1935. Only then, on their fifth try, did they finally win a World Series.

The Tigers beat the Cubs in the 1935 Series. Tigers outfielder Pete Fox starred in the six-game series. He hit .385 with three doubles, a triple, and four RBIs. Pitchers Tommy Bridges and Schoolboy Rowe were dominant, too. They combined to strike out 23 batters in 39 innings. The hometown fans were so happy that they

Mickey Cochrane crosses home plate in the ninth inning of Game 7 of the 1935 World Series. His run secured the Tigers' first championship.

refused to leave Navin Field in Detroit even hours after the game ended.

Like many cities during that era, Detroit was struggling with the Great Depression. The World Series victory was one of the best things to happen to the city in a long time. Eventually, Cochrane spoke to the crowd, begging them to go home. They finally obeyed, but the 1935 Detroit Tigers remained heroes for years to come.

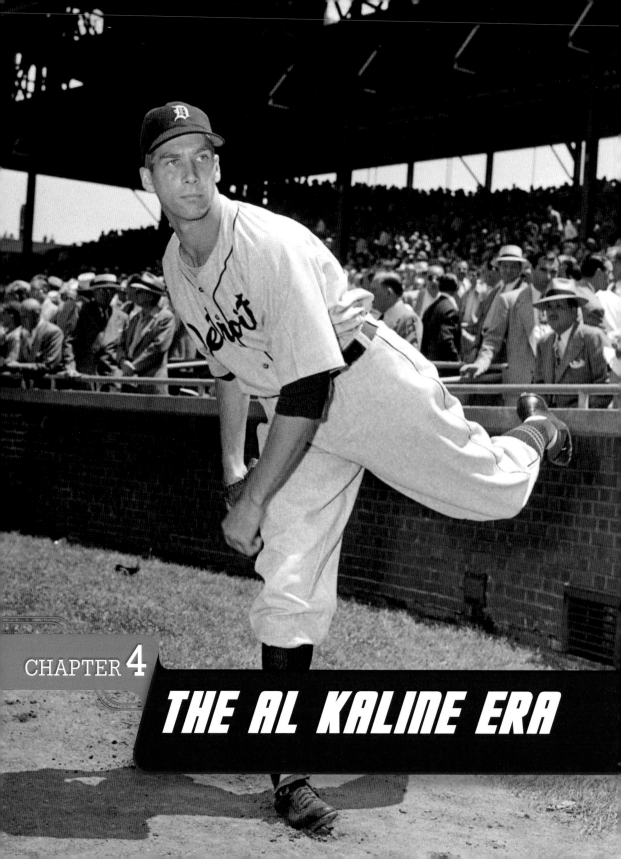

CHAPTER 4

THE AL KALINE ERA

The Tigers continued to be one of the best teams in the AL throughout the 1940s. This was largely thanks to players like infielder/outfielder Hank Greenberg and left-handed pitcher Hal Newhouser. Greenberg hit lots of home runs and was the AL MVP in 1935 and 1940. Newhouser was a league leader in strikeouts and wins en route to being named the 1944 and 1945 MVP.

Those two players also played a big role in the Tigers' win over the Chicago Cubs in the 1945 World Series. Greenberg batted .304, hit two home runs, and drove in seven runs in the seven-game series. Newhouser won two of the three games he started and struck out 22 batters. It was the Tigers' second World Series title. It would take the Tigers 23 years to win another one.

A lot of changes happened in the coming years. New players became stars. Third

Hal Newhouser warms up before a 1940 game against the New York Yankees. He developed into a two-time AL MVP.

baseman George Kell won the 1949 batting title on the last day of the season. Pitchers such as Virgil Trucks and Newhouser owned the mound. But the Tigers still turned into a losing team.

The 1952 Tigers lost 104 games. That was the most losses in team history. The 1953 season did not get much better. The Tigers lost 94 games.

Al Kaline

Al Kaline rose from a shy high school kid from Baltimore to one of the best outfielders in baseball history. He joined the Tigers in 1953. In 1955, he became the youngest player to win the AL batting title. Kaline twice finished second for the AL MVP Award. He played for the Tigers until his retirement in 1974. The team retired his No. 6 in 1980, making him the first Tiger to have his number retired. He also entered the Baseball Hall of Fame in 1980. Kaline remained with the Tigers after he retired from the playing field, working as a broadcaster and then as a special assistant.

The Tigers made a lot of trades after that. They even traded away star players such as Kell in an effort to build a winning team. But the player they needed the most was already on the team: outfielder Al Kaline.

Kaline came to the Tigers in 1953. He became one of the first high school players to jump straight to the major leagues without spending time in the minors. Kaline was only 18 years old. The skinny ballplayer looked very much like a kid. He was once stopped from entering the Tigers' clubhouse during his early years. A security guard at Briggs Stadium did not believe Kaline was old enough to be a player.

But Kaline dazzled with his talent. He was an excellent hitter and very good in the outfield. He was also quite polite and a bit shy. Kaline was

Al Kaline, shown in 1959, spent 22 seasons with the Tigers and was selected to the All-Star Game 15 times.

content to learn from the older players. As he developed into one of the best players in team history, the Tigers became a winning team once again.

Kaline—along with pitchers Mickey Lolich and Denny McLain and sluggers Norm Cash and Willie Horton—led the 1967 Tigers. They nearly

THE VOICE OF THE TIGERS

One of the most popular Detroit Tigers of all time never actually played for the team. Radio and television broadcaster Ernie Harwell was as famous as the Tigers' biggest stars. He broadcast Tigers games from 1960 until 2002, making him a big part of the team for generations of fans.

Harwell was known for a few distinctive phrases during games. For a strikeout where the player was caught looking: "He stood there like the house by the side of the road and watched it go by." For home runs: "That's looooong gone!" For double plays: "That's two for the price of one."

Harwell was inducted into the Baseball Hall of Fame in 1981. He died on May 4, 2010, at age 92. His death was mourned by fans and the Detroit Tigers alike. Part of his memorial was held at Comerica Park, allowing fans to say good-bye.

guided the team all the way back to the World Series. The Tigers lost the AL pennant on the last day of the season. The AL champion Boston Red Sox went to the World Series.

The disappointment stuck with the Tigers. The players vowed to do better in 1968. And they kept their word. The 1968 Tigers went 103–59 to win the AL pennant. They faced a familiar foe in the World Series: the St. Louis Cardinals. It was a very evenly matched World Series, with both teams playing well.

After six games the Series was tied. The teams played a decisive Game 7 at St. Louis. Cardinals pitcher Bob Gibson was on the mound. He had won his last seven World Series starts heading into Game 7. Meanwhile, Tigers pitcher Lolich was still a bit tired from pitching three days earlier.

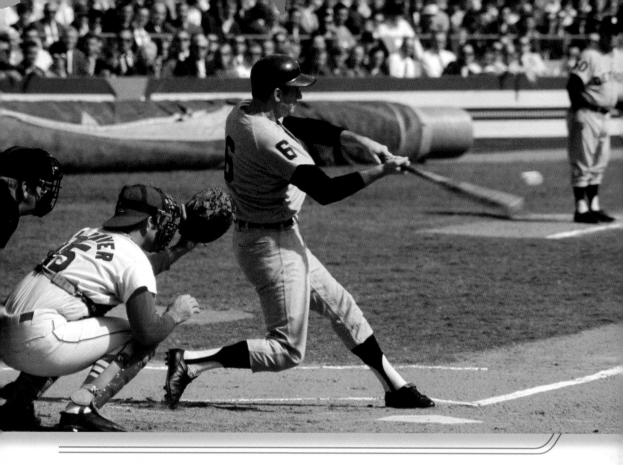

Tigers outfielder Al Kaline hits the ball against the St. Louis Cardinals during the 1968 World Series. The Tigers won the Series in seven games.

But Lolich proved to be stronger. He held the Cardinals scoreless until the ninth inning. Their one run in the ninth was not enough. The Tigers won the game 4–1 to clinch their third World Series title. Once again, the city of Detroit threw a big party to celebrate another dramatic World Series victory.

Denny McLain

Pitcher Denny McLain twice won the AL Cy Young Award. He was also one of only 13 pitchers to win 30 games in a season. But McLain had a colorful personality. Off the field, he liked to record albums and give organ concerts. He also drank a case of cola each day and did other things that made managers angry. He retired in 1972 due to an arm injury.

CHAPTER 5

THE ROAR OF '84

After the 1968 World Series, the Tigers managed to reach the 1972 ALCS. But that high soon faded away. The Tigers turned average during the rest of the 1970s, winning as many games as they lost. By 1979, the team was in need of a change. They found it in the form of new manager Sparky Anderson.

Anderson had helped the Cincinnati Reds win the World Series in 1975 and 1976. Now he wanted to do the same with the Tigers. He took over a Tigers team that had many young players. Some had only recently come up from the minors. Anderson soon helped turn some of them into stars.

Pitcher Jack Morris, shortstop Alan Trammell, second baseman Lou Whitaker, catcher Lance Parrish, and outfielder Kirk Gibson had all joined the team between 1977 and 1979. Anderson worked with the players, teaching them how to work hard and become winners. The results soon showed.

Manager Sparky Anderson revitalized the Tigers after coming to Detroit for the 1979 season.

SPARKY ANDERSON

Longtime Tigers manager Sparky Anderson was known as much for his managerial skills as he was for his superstitions. Anderson never stepped on the baseline when he made trips to the mound. He followed the same pattern every day: having breakfast, going for a walk, and taking a nap before games.

Anderson also said interesting things: "If I ever find a pitcher who has heat, a good curve, and a slider, I might seriously consider marrying him, or at least proposing." And: "Me carrying a briefcase is like a hot dog wearing earrings."

Anderson retired in 1995, and was inducted into the Hall of Fame in 2000. He is the winningest manager in the histories of both the Tigers and the Cincinnati Reds.

By 1984, the Tigers had one of the most talented teams in baseball. They were able to turn that talent into one of the most dominant seasons in baseball history. The 1984 Tigers began the season 35–5. That was the best record any team had ever had over the first 40 games of a season. They never let up for the rest of the year. The Tigers led the AL East from the first day of the season to the last. Until 1984, only the legendary 1927 New York Yankees had accomplished that feat.

Whitaker and Trammell proved to be the core of the team. Both were top fielders and the two players turned many double plays together.

Tigers pitcher Jack Morris was 19–11 with a 3.60 earned run average during the 1984 season. He also won all three games he pitched during the postseason.

They also had strong seasons at the plate. Trammell batted .314, while Whitaker was at .289. Meanwhile, Parrish led the team with 33 home runs and 98 RBIs.

Gibson was a fan favorite. He had grown up in Detroit and played baseball and football at Michigan State. He drove in 91 runs while stealing a team-high 29 bases.

Morris anchored a strong pitching staff. The workhorse pitcher struck out 148 batters and compiled a 19–11 record. But the star of the pitching staff was Willie Hernandez. The Tigers' closer saved 32 games with an earned run average (ERA) of only 1.92. He was not only the 1984 Cy Young Award winner; he was also the 1984 AL MVP.

It was an overall dominant season in Detroit. The Tigers had six All-Stars—Parrish, Trammell, Whitaker, outfielder Chet Lemon, Hernandez, and Morris. Parrish, Trammell, and Whitaker all won AL Gold Gloves. Parrish and Whitaker also added AL Silver Slugger Awards as the best batters at their positions. To cap it off, Anderson was named the AL Manager of the Year.

The Tigers finished the season 104–58. That was an astonishing 15 games better than the second-place Toronto Blue Jays in the AL East. The

Dynamic Duo

They became known simply by their nicknames: "Tram" and "Sweet Lou." Shortstop Alan Trammell and second baseman Lou Whitaker were the heart of the Tigers infield from 1977 to 1995. Trammell, who retired after the 1996 season, joined Al Kaline and Ty Cobb as the only Tigers to play 20 or more years for the team. The duo played 1,918 games together, turning more than 1,200 double plays.

Alan Trammell, *left*, Willie Hernandez, *center*, and Darrell Evans celebrate after the Tigers beat the Kansas City Royals in the 1984 ALCS.

Tigers' record was 20 games better than that of the AL West champion Kansas City Royals. But since the Royals won their division, they met the Tigers in the ALCS.

The Tigers won Game 1 by a score of 8–1. But the Royals kept it close after that. The Tigers needed extra-innings to win Game 2. The Royals then held the Tigers to only one run

The Journeymen

Manager Sparky Anderson was known for his ability to get the most out of every player. Even role players, such as outfielder Rusty Kuntz, catcher Marty Castillo, and outfielder Ruppert Jones played key roles during the 1984 season. Kuntz had the game-winning RBI on a sacrifice fly in Game 5 of the World Series. Castillo, who was not known to be a good hitter, hit .333 in the World Series. Jones batted a career-high .284 that season and hit 12 home runs.

in Game 3. But that was enough for the Tigers; they won 1–0.

The Tigers faced the NL champion San Diego Padres in the World Series. The hometown outfielder, Gibson, came up big at the biggest time.

Game 1 was in San Diego. The Padres were down 3–2 in the seventh when utility player Kurt Bevacqua tried to stretch a double into a triple. A triple would have put him in good position to tie the game. But Gibson's throw from right field got Bevacqua out at third. The Tigers held on to win 3–2.

The Tigers came into Game 5 at Tiger Stadium with a 3–1 series lead. After the top of the eighth, they led by a score of 5–4. Then, with two outs in the bottom of the eighth, Gibson stepped to the plate against Padres ace reliever Goose Gossage. Gibson proceeded to smash a three-run home run to the upper deck in right field. As he ran around the bases, he famously pumped his fist, then raised his arms, and finally jumped up and down after he crossed home. With an 8–4 lead and lots of momentum, the World Series title was in sight.

Hernandez came in for the top of the ninth to close out the

Hometown Hero

Kirk Gibson was a top receiver for the Michigan State football team. His coach suggested Gibson also try out for the Spartans baseball team. Gibson played one season of baseball, hitting .390. He impressed scouts so much that he was drafted to play professionally in both sports. The Tigers selected him to play baseball while the St. Louis Cardinals football team selected him to play in the National Football League. He chose to play baseball. Manager Sparky Anderson worked with Gibson, making him into a more disciplined player. The results were seen during the 1984 season, when Gibson led with his defense and hitting.

Kirk Gibson belts his first of two home runs during the fifth game of the 1984 World Series. His second home run sealed the Series for the Tigers.

Series. Just like that, the Tigers were World Series champions once more. It was a special win for Anderson. He became the first manager to win the World Series with both an AL and an NL team. But it was a special moment that would have to last a long time for Tigers fans. They are still trying to add a fifth championship.

CHAPTER 6

FROM LOW TO HIGH

T he Tigers only had a few more years of success after winning the 1984 World Series. They overcame the Toronto Blue Jays to win the AL East in a dramatic ending to the 1987 season. But then the Minnesota Twins proved to be too much in the ALCS.

The players who had starred for the Tigers in 1984 were beginning to leave the team. Catcher Lance Parrish had left before the 1987 season. Outfielder Kirk Gibson left afterward. By 1989, the Tigers were a shadow of their former selves. The 1989 Tigers lost 103 games. Manager Sparky Anderson became ill during the season and had to leave the Tigers for a while.

Debate also started about the fate of Tiger Stadium. The ballpark had stood in one form or another in the same location since 1912. But it was starting to fall apart. The Tigers were falling apart, too. Anderson

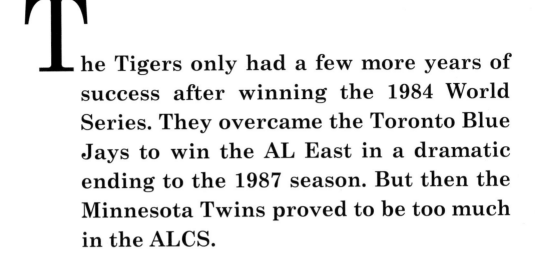

First baseman Cecil Fielder starred for the Tigers from 1990 to 1996. He led the league twice in home runs and three times in RBIs in that time.

retired at the end of the 1995 season.

The Tigers slid into losing seasons for years. They lost more games than they won from 1994 through 2005. Although MLB expanded the playoffs in 1995, the Tigers did not make the playoffs once. Meanwhile, Tiger Stadium closed on September 27, 1999, with the Tigers winning one last time.

The Tigers moved into Comerica Park for the 2000 season. But the new setting did not bring better baseball. Two of the Tigers' worst seasons ever were to come. In 2002, the Tigers lost 106 games. The team fired two managers during that one season.

Things were even worse in 2003. Alan Trammell had been one of the stars of the 1984 World Series championship team. But as the Tigers' manager, the team lost 119 games. It was the worst record in team history, and nearly the worst record ever. Trammell lasted two more seasons before he was fired in 2005.

The Tigers hired Jim Leyland to take over as manager for the 2006 season. He brought a new, winning attitude to the team. The Tigers

Comerica Park

Comerica Park in downtown Detroit holds 41,000 people in its two decks. It features statues of famous players, such as Ty Cobb, Charlie Gehringer, Hank Greenberg, Willie Horton, Al Kaline, and Hal Newhouser in the right field concourse. Another statue of broadcaster Ernie Harwell is located on the concourse behind home plate. Large, pouncing Tigers, made of concrete, stand at the ballpark's main entrance. There is also a merry-go-round and baseball-themed Ferris wheel in the concourse. The main scoreboard, which is 180 feet (54.9 m) wide, has two big tigers perched on each side. The tigers' eyes glow red during night games.

Eric Munson, *right*, and Craig Paquette, *left*, leave the dugout after the Tigers lost their ninth consecutive game to start the 2003 season.

also began adding established stars like Magglio Ordonez, Kenny Rogers, Ivan Rodriguez, and Placido Polanco. The team quickly began a turnaround.

Two rookie pitchers played a big role in that turnaround. Justin Verlander was named AL Rookie of the Year after going 17–9 with a 3.63 ERA in 2006.

Reliever Joel Zumaya was among the hardest throwing pitchers in the league. He had 97 strikeouts in 83.1 innings with a 1.94 ERA as a setup man.

The Tigers had a scare late in the season, though. After a hot start, they had a losing record in their last 50 games. Then, in the final game of the season, the Twins surpassed them to win the AL Central. But the Tigers finished 95–67. That was good enough to earn them the team's first wild-card berth into the playoffs. It was the first time since 1987 that the Tigers were part of the playoffs.

Detroit was a happy baseball town again. The Tigers beat the New York Yankees in the AL Division Series. The celebration in Comerica Park lasted for a long time. The fans cheered, and the players returned the love by standing on the dugouts and spraying champagne on them. Then they beat the Oakland Athletics in the ALCS.

Although the Tigers lost to the St. Louis Cardinals in the 2006 World Series, hope returned in Detroit.

Verlander continued pitching well after his rookie season. He even threw a no-hitter— the first in Comerica Park and the sixth in Tigers history—on June 12, 2007. He struck out 12 Milwaukee Brewers in the 4–0 win. The Tigers traded for

Spring Training

The Tigers have called Lakeland, Florida their spring training home since 1934. "Tiger Town," which stretches over 12 acres, has been improved over the years to fit the Tigers' needs. The Tigers briefly left Tiger Town from 1943 to 1945 to train in Evansville, Indiana. But they came back for good in 1946. Joker Marchant Stadium, the main playing field, was built in 1966. There is a dormitory for players, offices, and ball fields for practice.

Justin Verlander pitches against the Los Angeles Angels in 2006. Verlander was the AL Rookie of the Year that season.

first baseman Miguel Cabrera after the 2007 season. He and Ordonez became the Tigers' main sluggers.

Cabrera, Ordonez, and Verlander almost led the Tigers back to the playoffs in 2009. The Tigers played well all season.

ALMOST PERFECT

The Tigers' Armando Galarraga was one out away from pitching a perfect game on June 2, 2010. To complete it, he just had to retire Cleveland Indians shortstop Jason Donald. Donald grounded to Tigers first baseman Miguel Cabrera. Galarraga ran to cover first base. Cabrera's throw clearly beat Donald for the final out—and the perfect game. But umpire Jim Joyce called Donald safe. Everybody was stunned.

However, Galarraga did not complain. After the game, Joyce apologized to the pitcher and they shared a hug. The next day, Galarraga delivered the Tigers' lineup card to Joyce and the two men shook hands at home plate. Many commended Galarraga for his sportsmanship, including Joyce. "[He] will always be remembered for his grace and class, regardless of what the record books say," Joyce said when the two presented an award together at the ESPYs award show.

They even led the AL Central for 146 days. But as they had done in 2006, they slumped toward the end of the season. After 162 games, the Tigers and Twins were tied for first place.

The Tigers traveled to Minnesota for a deciding Game 163. But the Tigers lost 6–5 in 12 innings. The Tigers had missed the playoffs again. The team entered the 2010 season looking like it could again contend for the division title. But a barrage of midseason injuries kept them short.

Tigers fans were disappointed, but were left with the same feeling that's guided them for more than 100 years: there's always next year.

Tigers designated hitter Carlos Guillen congratulates first baseman Miguel Cabrera after Cabrera scored during a 2010 game. Cabrera led the AL in RBIs that season.

TIMELINE

1881	The Detroit Wolverines join the NL. They later become known as the Creams, and then the Tigers.
1901	The Tigers play for the first time in the AL on April 25. They win, 14–13, over the Milwaukee Brewers at Bennett Field in Detroit.
1905	Ty Cobb plays his first game for the Tigers on August 30. He would go on to play 2,806 games over 22 years with the team.
1907	The Tigers win their first AL pennant, but after tying the first game they lost the next four World Series games to the Chicago Cubs.
1908	The Tigers lose the World Series again to the Cubs, again in five games.
1909	The Tigers lose the World Series for a third straight year, this time in seven games to the Pittsburgh Pirates.
1934	The Tigers lose another World Series in seven games, this time to the St. Louis Cardinals.
1935	Finally, after four defeats, the Tigers win their first World Series, defeating the Cubs in six games.
1940	The Cincinnati Reds beat the Tigers in seven games to win the World Series.
1945	The Tigers win the second World Series title in team history, beating the Cubs in seven games.

1948	The Tigers play their first night game at home on June 15, defeating the Philadelphia Athletics 4–1.
1960	Ernie Harwell, future Baseball Hall of Famer, begins broadcasting Tigers games.
1968	The Tigers win a third World Series title, beating the Cardinals in seven games.
1984	The Tigers win their fourth World Series, at Tiger Stadium, over the San Diego Padres.
1987	The Minnesota Twins defeat the Tigers in five games to win the AL pennant.
1999	The last game played at Tiger Stadium, a Tigers win over the Kansas City Royals, takes place on September 27.
2000	The Tigers play their first game in Comerica Park on April 11, a win over the Seattle Mariners.
2002	Harwell calls his last Tigers game on September 29, ending a 42-year career with the team.
2003	The Tigers lose 119 games, one shy of tying the worst record in MLB history.
2006	The Tigers reach the World Series, but lose to the Cardinals in five games.
2010	Harwell dies at age 92.

QUICK STATS

FRANCHISE HISTORY
Detroit Wolverines (1881–88)
Detroit Tigers (1901–)

WORLD SERIES
(wins in bold)
1907, 1908, 1909, 1934, **1935**, 1940, **1945**, **1968**, **1984**, 2006

AL CHAMPIONSHIP SERIES
(1969–)
1972, 1984, 1987, 2006

DIVISION CHAMPIONSHIPS
(1969–)
1972, 1984, 1987

KEY PLAYERS
(position[s]; seasons with team)
Norm Cash (1B; 1960–74)
Ty Cobb (OF; 1905–26)
Sam Crawford (OF/IF; 1903–17)
Charlie Gehringer (2B; 1924–42)

Kirk Gibson (OF/DH; 1979–87, 1993–95)
Hank Greenberg (1B/OF; 1930, 1933–41, 1945–46)
Harry Heilmann (OF/IF; 1914, 1916–29)
Al Kaline (OF; 1953–74)
George Kell (3B; 1946–52)
Jack Morris (SP; 1977–90)
Hal Newhouser (P; 1939–53)
Schoolboy Rowe (P; 1933–42)
Alan Trammell (SS; 1977–96)
Lou Whitaker (2B; 1977–95)
Justin Verlander (SP; 2005–)

KEY MANAGERS
Sparky Anderson (1979–95): 1,331–1,248; 8–5 (postseason)
Hughie Jennings (1907–20): 1,131–972; 4–12 (postseason)

HOME PARKS
Bennett Field (1896–1911)
    Known as Bennett Park (1896–1900)
Tiger Stadium (1912–99)
    Known as Navin Field (1912–37), Briggs Stadium (1938–60)
Comerica Park (2000–)

* All statistics through 2010 season

QUOTES AND ANECDOTES

Tigers slugger Willie Horton grew up in Detroit. He got to play in Tiger Stadium for the first time at age 14 during a high school all-star game. Horton hit a home run during the game, and was shocked. "It scared me so much the umpire had to tell me to run," Horton said.

Tigers pitcher Mark "The Bird" Fidrych did things on the mound that had never been seen before. He talked to the baseball. He patted the dirt down on the mound with his hands before every inning, like he was gardening. He was nicknamed "The Bird" after Big Bird on *Sesame Street*, because he was tall and had blond hair. His best season was in 1976, when he had a 19–9 record and a 2.34 ERA. He was the AL Rookie of the Year. The next year, Fidrych hurt his knee and arm and was not able to pitch well anymore. But for one magical season, "The Bird" was the big star.

Tigers manager Hughie Jennings liked to study. He studied players. He studied teams. And he also studied in school. Jennings went to Cornell University and graduated with a law degree. He worked as a lawyer in the off-season, and clearly also brought his smarts to the baseball field. He managed the Tigers from 1907 to 1920, helping the team win three pennants. Jennings liked to have fun, kicking up his leg high in the air, tossing clumps of grass, and yelling "Ee-yah!" while he coached at third base. He thought it helped the Tigers to hit and score.

It was easy for the Tigers to figure out what they should pick for a mascot: a tiger. The Tigers mascot, PAWS, appears at every game at Comerica Park. He debuted May 5, 1995. PAWS entertains during games by playing jokes on fans and dancing on the dugouts. According to the team, PAWS likes to vacation in Lakeland, Florida and collects baseball cards for a hobby.

GLOSSARY

ace

A team's best pitcher.

berth

A place, spot, or position, such as in the baseball playoffs.

clinch

To officially settle something, such as a berth in the playoffs.

contend

To be in the race for a championship or playoff berth.

designated hitter

A position used only in the American League. Managers can employ an extra hitter in the batting order who comes to the plate to hit instead of the pitcher.

franchise

An entire sports organization, including the players, coaches, and staff.

mediocre

Neither good nor bad.

momentum

A continued strong performance based on recent success.

pennant

A flag. In baseball, it symbolizes that a team has won its league championship.

postseason

The games in which the best teams play after the regular-season schedule has been completed.

retire

To officially end one's career.

rookie

A first-year player in the major leagues.

veteran

An individual with great experience in a particular endeavor.

wild card

Playoff berths given to the best remaining teams that did not win their respective divisions.

FOR MORE INFORMATION

Further Reading

Bak, Richard. *A Place for Summer: A Narrative History of Tiger Stadium.* Detroit, MI: Wayne State University Press, 1998.

Harwell, Ernie. *The Babe Signed My Shoe: Tales of the Grand Old Game.* South Bend, IN: Diamond Communications, 1994.

Lieb, Frederick. *The Detroit Tigers.* Kent, OH: The Kent State University Press, 2008.

Web Links

To learn more about the Detroit Tigers, visit ABDO Publishing Company online at **www.abdopublishing.com**. Web sites about the Tigers are featured on our Book Links page. These links are routinely monitored and updated to provide the most current information available.

Places to Visit

Comerica Park
2100 Woodward Avenue
Detroit, MI 48201-3470
313-962-4000
mlb.mlb.com/det/ballpark/index.jsp
This has been the Tigers' home field since 2000. The team plays 81 regular-season games here each year. Tours are available when the Tigers are not playing.

National Baseball Hall of Fame and Museum
25 Main Street
Cooperstown, NY 13326
888-HALL-OF-FAME
www.baseballhall.org
This hall of fame and museum highlights the greatest players and moments in the history of baseball. Ty Cobb, Hank Greenberg, Al Kaline, and manager Sparky Anderson are among the former Tigers enshrined there.

Tiger Town
2301 Lakeland Hills Blvd.
Lakeland, FL 33805
863-686-8075
mlb.mlb.com/det/ballpark/
springtraining.jsp
Tiger Town has been the Tigers' spring-training home since 1934.

INDEX

About the Author

Joanne C. Gerstner is an award-winning sports journalist. Her work has appeared in the *New York Times*, *USA Today*, the *Miami Herald,* and the *Detroit News* over the past 15 years. She also appears on ESPN as an expert guest. Gerstner has covered the biggest sporting events in the world, reporting from the Olympics, the World Cup, the tennis and golf US Opens, the NBA Finals, the Stanley Cup Finals, and the Super Bowl. She grew up in Detroit, loving the Tigers and the Red Wings.